MW00606987

MASK OFF

LOIS MILIKNI

COPYRIGHT

Hardcover ISBN: 978-1-957751-47-4

eBook ISBN: 978-1-957751-48-1

Edited by: Nicole Evans

First Hardcover edition, 2023

JOURNAL JOY

An *Imprint* of Journal Joy *Publishers*

www.thejournaljoy.com

DEDICATION

I dedicated my book to God First! Without him I'm nothing!

To myself Because I'm a survivor and I put in the work to make the well-needed changes for growth!

To my ride or die! my mutha fucking sister Qutoni (Qu Tee) for riding this roller coaster of life with me!

She's had my back a million percent!

I can't stress enough how much I love her and adore her love for me!

Saying I'm grateful is an understatement!

To my momma NELVIDA for showing me how to survive in this crazy world: Embedding Strength in me and teaching me how to pray and trust God!

To my Daddy Ray who loves me and adored me!

Nothing I did disappoint him!

To my children Jason Jr. and Jasmine BARTLOW who loved me unconditionally, with no judgments, I thank God for my babies!

Also, Rannete chase my bestie Naiena's momma for finding me and getting me out of California in hopes to save my life!

My other ride or die! My Bitch / Best friend Naenia, that's my A1! Since Day 1!

My other two besties Charlene Crawford and Tammy Torrance!

I love and miss them dearly! RIH Queens.

To my niece Ices, thank you for always loving me even when you were old enough to see the real me!

My nephews Bubba and Dootie, y'all always said Auntie you got this, we love you!!

Last but not least, my king! I love him and appreciate him with my whole soul. Our love is timeless! Love always, your unicorn.

CONTENTS

MASK OFF

Today April 6th, 2021 is the day I decided to share my story with the love of my life. It started sort of like this: Daddy, I need to share my testimony with you! I had his full attention. He was all ears, and my insides started trembling, but I knew it was time! King is one of a kind, but I said this can either make us or break us!

I spoke my truth.

He looked at me in my soul and said it's ok, it doesn't define who you are. Man, I couldn't ask for a better soul. Our mind plays tricks on us, let me tell you. But King is the real deal. Well today, we awakened and in my flesh I was embarrassed, but in my spiritual side, I knew I had to follow my heart. Those who matter to me know I'm as free as I've ever felt in my 46 years. I told myself when I met him he would be my husband for life. Now listen and learn what led to this.

Hey princess, I'm sorry for abandoning you! As I type this the tears won't stop falling down my cheeks. I had no idea that one day that little girl would need me. You see all I knew is that I had to save myself, not knowing she was a part of me. I was just a baby when I was being violated by my uncle and cousins. It was painful to keep this secret. I was told if I said something they were going to do the same thing to my little sister! I couldn't let that happen! My sister was my everything, I didn't know what I'd do without her. She always made me feel like I wasn't alone. I was being physically and mentally abused. I remember being four years old and my mom telling me that I was fast, and sitting my ass down. But in reality, all I was doing was dressing up in her clothes, heels, and mink coats. I had no idea what being fast was! Dressing in her clothes and heels was my happy place. I loved fashion then and I am obsessed with it now! Ha, I keep speaking to myself, saying Lois it's not too late. I can do whatever I put my mind to.

I've been in survival mode for over a few decades. This lady had become tired, and all she wanted to do was ease the pain she carried all this time unknowingly and unwillingly. I found myself looking for love in all the wrong places. When all I had to do was love myself.

At age 12 my grandmother died from Cancer even though it took some time to take over her life, as a little girl it felt as if it happened suddenly. She was my protector. No one in this world ever made me feel safe, besides my daddy or my grandmother. And at the time Daddy was in San Quentin State Prison. What was I to do??? Who do I now turn to? I felt all alone! I was vulnerable and unprotected, and I sat there screaming and crying, what am I going to do? A few months later when grandmother's house was cleaned and cleared out, my mama moved us to deep East Oakland 92nd and Sunnyside.

A few days later I met the man that nine years after meeting him, I would have the most beautiful child I could have ever been blessed with, my son. Jason Jr., Twelve months later I gave birth to the most amazing little girl. Jazmine. I said God must really love me and that he would trust me with these innocent angels. I had no idea how to love. I never knew what loving myself consisted of, so how could I love them? I was hard on myself as I was trying to be the best mother possible.

Fast forward. A few years later around 16 years of age I was attempting to numb myself. I started smoking weed, drinking hard liquor, and started playing around with powder which resulted in me going even deeper. I started sprinkling powder in my weed which eventually led to smoking it. I didn't think much of it because back then all the ones I considered bosses were doing the same thing.

I had gotten introduced to it while indulging in some freaky shit. Ha, but I knew that it wasn't me. I couldn't really enjoy it. My flesh was frozen, but the pain didn't go away. It was just a temporary avoidance, and after a while, it got out of control. As I type, these tears won't stop falling! Every time I heard this one song play, how did I get here?

"Nobody's supposed to be here"...

by DEBORAH COX. It me deep down in my soul because it's a question I asked myself

See, my consciousness and self-love were hitting me hard. I was being raped and sold for drugs, and it wasn't my choice. I was afraid. Scared for my life one day, I was on my normal routine of getting high to numb my deep-rooted pain, this guy pulled up on me to take a ride with him and smoke/drink all I wanted. Not knowing this nigga had his own agenda! That night I was kidnapped and raped he took me to Oakland Hills. I remember escaping by stabbing that man! With a pipe, I had in my hand! I hopped out of that car and ran as fast as I could, screaming, thank you, Jesus, thank you, Jesus! As I raced through the hills, there was a car following me. Although I moved quickly, it seemed like the car had been tailing me for a decade. As I got closer to Oakland Zoo on Stanley Avenue and 98th I knew I was almost to my children. I kept telling myself, I was safe!

In the car that was following me was a lady who raised her window down and kept asking me, "Baby are you ok"? I was so upset, angered, and afraid I had no idea she was checking on my safety until I reached my destination.

Man looking back, God had a plan for me. In the neighborhood, there were four of us, my sister, Qutoni, my brothers Taskeen, Jasper, and I. Qu was the fighter in the family. I was the one who wanted to love everyone lol! I loved making little girls feel pretty by dressing them up and letting my sister do their hair. Then there are my little brothers; man, they were so bad always getting into trouble. As I'm older I now understand why they acted out the way they did. We were all physically abused by momma.

My momma started having more kids. By the time I was twelve, she had my little sister, Davida.

After Vida, she gave birth to Lydia. The following year she had my youngest brother DeEnd whom we call number seven. He was the seventh child, and momma named him DeEnd because she said he would definitely be the last one! (The end.) lol, momma did have a sense of humor. I was the oldest.

Let me take you back. Before all the drugs I had always been known as the pretty, chocolate, long hair beauty. I truly couldn't wrap my head around why momma kept having all these kids! This world was so cruel. And let me be honest she would leave us home for hours that turned into days. I remember living directly across the street on 69th St. village in East Oakland in a green and White House.

Momma had been gone for a few days. She made my sister, Qu, my brothers Taz, Jaz and myself lock ourselves up in a bedroom with a small refrigerator in it. All I remember is us having Vienna sausage, top ramen, and milk which I hate to this day! And at that time I was five or six years old. Such a huge responsibility for such a young child.

As I look back, I wonder how I was even able to take care of these kids when I was a kid myself.

It was a few days before Daddy got back in town and found us there alone, He was furious. Later that night when momma pulled up in front of the house, hopping out of the car. I said to myself when I saw her coming into the house, which man was she with this time? She always kept a man no matter what.

Momma walked in that door as if nothing happened! Daddy started screaming and hollering, "Nell, why did you leave these kids in here like this"? You see, momma ran all the other men in her life! and beat them up.

Momma didn't play, but on this day Daddy wasn't playing with her! She started screaming at Qu and me to get the Butcher knife out of the kitchen. Although we were scared of Momma and did everything she told us with no questions asked. We weren't going to assist momma this time, he was our daddy! So momma tried to fight daddy. Daddy wasn't having it. He picked up that old-school speaker you used to see in the 70s and 80s and put it right on top of momma's head.

She still has that scar. As I reflect on that incident, my daddy didn't play when it came to us., and that made me feel safe. Daddy handled the lady we were terrified of. And he didn't leave quite as often as he used to. I remember Daddy taking me to kindergarten. There was this little boy that had a huge crush on me. He kept asking me to be his girlfriend. I was disgusted with that idea, so I went home one day and told Daddy, he kept bothering me.

Daddy took me to school the next day. Oh how I miss my daddy, he was my hero. As we walked up 69th Street towards my school which was on the corner of 69th and E14th, he had me on his shoulders. I was filled with joy. He took me to class and asked to speak with Tyrone. If I tell you to this day I don't know what Daddy told him, but he never bothered me again.

I don't blame him, because my dad was very intimidating. Daddy was huge in muscle, and he was known as one of the strongest men in San Quentin.

I remember Daddy going back to jail. I was eight years old, living on 48th and Shattuck, North Oakland, off of Shattuck. When I think back to those days, there were some good, but lots of bad days. Momma always ran the streets, and we used to get dropped off at Grandmother Lois' house on 63rd and Racine. There were many fun times, more fun than bad I thought.

Unfortunately, I was used to getting molested. I hated it, but I also hated getting beat and feeling like I wasn't good enough by and for my momma.

One day momma was home. I was playing outside and got called into the house. Momma called me there. I don't recall what I did but momma beat me with a plunger! I was only seven or eight years old as soon as I could escape, I ran to Caspers hot dog stand up the street on the corner of Shattuck. I used the first pay phone I saw and called 911! I called the police on Momma.

I remember thinking they could save me. To my surprise when they arrived I spoke up and told them my mom had beaten me and the men in her family kept molesting me! Y'all know what?

They took me back to my mom's house. I just knew Mom was in trouble. They were gonna stop her from beating me and my siblings! To my surprise, momma opened the door, and the police asked her if I was her daughter. Mom said, yes. They asked her if she whipped me using a plunger and she said yes! She told the cops. And I'll do it again"! My little heart sank at that very moment. The cops looked down at my tiny frame and said, Lois, you have to listen to your mom. and then made me go back into that apartment! That's the day I lost all respect for the cops. I never put my trust in them again.

Back at Grandmother Lois' house, I was able to be a child. If Mom would think to yell or beat me, Grandma would put her out. There were times when momma would make me go home after she got yelled at, so it made me afraid at times. Then there were times, I was afraid to go to sleep at grandma's house when my uncles or guy cousins stayed over because I was awakened by their inappropriate fondling. There were definitely pros and cons to going there. It made me start hating men! I hated men for decades.

After my grandmother died we moved to East Oakland, on 92nd and Sunnyside. We were the new faces on the block. There were so many guys on Sunnyside. They were giving money to my brothers Taskeen and Jasper. Taskeen and Jasper were younger than me. They met a boy their age named Johnathan. We called him Lil John. He ended up being my BD's younger brother. These boys were so bad. One day they robbed the detail shop on Bancroft. They came flying down Sunnyside; it seemed as if they were doing one hundred miles an hour. It was lil' John and my brothers. They had to be the ages nine and ten years old. They stole all luxury cars, They never got caught.

On another day, lil' John's big brother came to Momma's house looking for him. He was this light-skinned brother that seemed different from the other guys on the block. There was something distinct about this guy. One day he just kept asking me what my name was. I was shy. I wondered what he wanted from me besides sex. You see I didn't even like guys. I was in the second grade when I knew I liked girls. It was just that I felt safe with them. But this guy seemed different. It was like the universe sent me another angel. Perhaps Grandma Lois sent me this angel. He made me feel safe with him. I was 12 years old, a virgin, and all the guys had a crush on me and my sister. They called us twins. We kept telling them we weren't twins. They said we were so gorgeous, with brown and caramel complexions, and they had choices. I actually fell in love with this guy. They called him J.B., short for Jason Bartlow. He was so kind back then. He spoiled me rotten, just like Daddy. He used to pay momma's rent. He draped me in the finest gold there was. And this is probably why I haven't really been into jewelry as an adult. He even let my momma use his red and white Oldsmobile Cutlass.

You see, Momma used to catch the 72 bus every day at 6 am for prayer at Ray Mack Church on 73rd E14t street, while she made us walk from 92nd and Sunnyside at 6 am for prayer. She even made us walk those streets with a big radio Raheem boombox speaker. We were embarrassed as hell! BD used to just look so sad watching me live like that.

I remember BD coming into Mommy's house while she was at Tuesday night bible study and he touched Momma's radio in the corner of our living room. My sister and I started yelling, please don't touch it!

You see, momma knew when that radio was touched. She had the knob positioned so only her eyes could see and tell. So yep, that's why he allowed her to use his car, so we wouldn't have to walk to places. Momma always made me hand over my jewelry to her, saying someone will cut my fingers off wearing all those diamonds! To this day at the age of 46, I asked her what she did with all of my jewelry.

I often laugh to myself because no answer has been explained, and it's just like her. I always dreamed of escaping that life at momma's house.

I never felt loved by her or that I was ever good enough for her to even notice me. One day she asked me if I loved BD. My stupid self said, "Yes, momma I love him!" She shook me dead in my eye. Right before she did it, my sister, Qu was hiding on the stairs and told me to run away! She must've seen it coming. I stood there afraid that if I did run, she would beat me, and she did beat me like a stranger off the street.

The next day BD saw me. I had one shoe on and the clothes on my back. He took me from momma's house that very day!! The crazy part is that his family lived right across the street. I mean you could throw a rock from my window at him. I was frightened, and he hid me in his mom's attic. I was there for over six months before Momma Bartlow even noticed... She left every day at 6 a.m. and returned a little after 10 p.m. When she closed the wash house, which she owned on 98th and Birch. I would come out of BD's attic every morning to return before Momma Bartlow got home.

One day momma sent the police to Ms. B's house. I was so afraid, I stayed in that basement trying not to breathe. I silently cried and prayed no one said anything, but BD wouldn't allow anyone to hurt me. I repeated this to myself in that incident... They didn't find me and that was one of my best days. I literally continued hiding for what seemed like an eternity.

Then to my surprise, we immediately moved to Seminary Avenue with one of BD's friends. I was only 14 years old and finally felt free. Before now I was never able to be a little girl. It's like I became an adult at five years old., But now I was living with my man, his friend, Donald, and his girl. That whole experience was something no 14-year-old child should be doing., I remember there was this girl named Sabrina. She was beautiful to me. She walked into the house with Donald's girlfriend, Teyana. I think BD saw the look on my face. I chuckled because I told him my secret: I liked girls...

9

Sabrina and I were smoking weed and drinking. We started kissing each other. The guys were gone, running the streets as they did daily, but it was getting late. I was nervous thinking they would return soon, but I couldn't resist the urge for her touch. To my amazement, BD wouldn't mind. We have played around with women since the day I had that experience. I kept telling myself maybe I should tell him. Something just wouldn't allow me to say it. By the time I turned 16 my baby's daddy introduced me to one of the baddest porn stars whose name I can't even remember right now. When I tell you I felt like I just reached heaven's doors on that 16th birthday, ha! Those were the days before shit went left.

At 19, I was pregnant with my young king, and I had him a month shy of turning 20. By the time lil Jay turned three months, I found out I was pregnant with my princess. I was so happy. I dreamed of having a boy and a girl and it came true back to back. By the time Jazz was born, we moved to a Sacramento area called Rancho Cordova. There, we tried to give the kids a better life than we had. Things started getting bad. I had a one-year-old and a newborn by the time I was 21. I had no idea what I was doing. It was hard but all I knew is to make shit happen. And that's exactly what I did. My children were my everything and still are. But who knew what mothering two innocent souls would consist of, when I wasn't nourished and didn't know how to love?

Everyone, I thought I should trust myself. I was obsessed with protecting my daughter, but it didn't come easily or naturally for me. I dreamed of being her best friend; her go-to person/mom. I was learning as I went along; never taught or shown how to love. And because of this, I later on found out I failed her. My son and I are closer, but I still crave that bond with my princess. I desired a strong and supportive relationship and truly hadn't lived or seen a healthy example of it. One day she will read this and hopefully understand, I just didn't know. I've given her material things I never had. She had a beautiful room, clothes, jewelry, and extravagant birthdays, but what she really desired from me, I absolutely had no clue how to give.

My childhood memory serves me very well and isn't all bad. I grew up getting two packs of cookies for a dollar on my birthdays and was very upset not realizing some kids had even less than me. Mom would draw and paint on our bedroom wall, creating all types of cartoon characters. And she's still creative in that way. What I didn't know as a little girl is that my mom went through similar experiences as I did growing up.

Fast forward to April 2021. It was Mom's birthday, and I was at Rodrick's house, in Richmond. Rodrick, my love-my king, I lived an hour away, but we hopped on the freeway to come to my sister Qu's house and celebrate my queen, momma. I asked one of our godbrothers to come to cook for Momma and we enjoyed a beautiful dinner. We were eating and laughed all night long. Music was playing in the background and an old-school song came on.

As I sang this song to her (whose title or words) I still can't remember, I started crying. She also started crying. The song connected our souls and we both felt it.

After that we were having shot after shot, something I slowed down on doing. When I drink I start to express myself. That night things got out of hand. Momma and I got into a big fight! I started yelling, "Don't Don't put your hands on me, I'm grown"!! Momma didn't care. It didn't seem to matter what was happening, but Mom always found a way to physically hurt me.

For example, after I found my dad deceased in his house I needed help and care. We were getting ready for Dad's funeral and Mom wanted money to go buy an outfit for Daddy's service.

I was mentally exhausted and couldn't comprehend anything at the moment. She slapped the shit out of me in front of all my family on Daddy's side and a few friends. At this time we were at my sister's Qu house, but she wasn't home... She was out getting Dad's obituary together. Things were a blur, but I remember my sister coming home and saying thank you, as tears ran down her cheeks. I looked up at her and asked her why she was saying thank you to me. Well due to us have said no one would hit us and get away with it ever again, she said she was happy I didn't tear up her house fighting momma back! I promised God I would never hit my mom, but that day in my flesh I wanted to hit her ass back! Lo and behold, three months before my 40th Birthday, momma struck again!

Rewind back to the night of momma Birthday celebration. I left my sister's home saying, "I'm done with that lady forever"! The next day my momma and sister pulled up to my door. I didn't want to open it, but my sister said, "sister I brought Mom here for a reason"., I opened that door, and it was no shocker, Mom asked me what she had done to me.? Tears started running down my face as I replied, "Why didn't you protect me, Mom"!!!!????

I looked at Momma and her response was, "I didn't know how". This response broke my heart at that moment. It's like my soul had just shattered into a million pieces. I was now almost 47 years old, wow, the number of completion. Momma said she didn't know how because my grandpa did it to her. Then I said you watched me suffer and never asked, or said anything to me? How is this possible? After that conversation with my momma, I decided to forgive her.

My mother never allowed anyone to hit or chastise us, so how was it normal for her to watch the pain in my eyes all of those years, and she didn't protect me from being molested?

On that date, 4/13/21 I understood she had no clue how to safeguard me, in my childhood years. I fought not to be like Momma and I turned out to be just like her. Momma was strong, had faith in God, never gave up, and was determined to survive. I said to myself yes, I am my mom. I've learned how to take the good from her and whatever I don't agree with I don't have to accept. I pray one day my daughter will see all the good in me! accept me for me, and forgive me for everything she feels I didn't do right.

I realized at just 24 years old that my mom loved me when she found me in a McDonald's. I was up all night partying with my drugs and I needed to wash myself up, so I went there. Surprisingly my mom walked in and said, "Lois I've been looking for you". I was ashamed, exhausted, and missing my children, but never wanted them, my siblings, or my mom, to see me like that!

Momma just hugged me, wiped my tears, and asked me if I was hungry, which I was./ We sat there talking and she asked me to go to church with her. I refused at the time, but when I tell y'all she never judged me, it would be an understatement.

Life started beating me up mentally. I had always swept things under the rug. All that garbage I kept hiding behind my smile caught up to me. I started hating myself. I was sleeping in cars. I couldn't figure out how to fight. I was numb. I'd been fighting forever., I just wanted to be free of all the pain. I was just stuck in a time zone. Why wasn't I fighting this demon in order to take care of my children? Why weren't they worth the fight?

One day I realized I had to fight for myself first! which I had never done before. I'm actually just recently learning how to do so. I had to love myself first. Those were very crazy days for me and the family that loved me.

I remember sleeping in the cars, thinking I was ready to end my own life, but there were these people walking down the street on E14th St. singing and praising God. Something told me to get out of the car. One lady said, "Let me pray for you. You're so beautiful and your light shines bright". I'm thinking to myself, wow… my angels had always been with me and she was one of them. I let her pray for me. I wept in guilt and shame, and she whispered it would be ok. I felt the angels that day as I feel them today.

After that prayer, I missed my kids dearly. I remember sitting in front of E Morris Cox Elementary School on 98th Ave. I could see my kids playing across the street in the wash house Ms. Barlow owned on 98th Ave. They couldn't see me.

I saw my children's father. He had been clean for a few months. He saw me and brought the kids across the street to where I'd been sitting crying my soul out, as I watched them playing and laughing. My babies ran across that street so happy to see me! I was glad to see them too., Jaz just ran into my arms.

She was about five at the time and lil' Jay was six. They made my day. We spent time together for a while, then I left. I was so deeply embarrassed to face reality. I just kept thinking everyone looked at me in disgust, the whole time.

That day I left my children. I just couldn't continue that way so, I called my sister, Qu, and told her I was tired. She drove from Sacramento and pulled up on Birch and 98th. I was ready. My children's father asked if he could come. My sister said no because she knew I needed to do this alone.

I hugged my children and got in the car. I was crying so hard and loudly. I didn't want to leave the city of Oakland. I knew I could normally just go over the hill and see them. Now it would take me over an hour plus. I'll be waiting for someone to give me a ride whenever they have time. These were some of the thoughts running through my head. But I had to make a choice and I did it for them!

This time I was leaving them two hours away! But I knew leaving them there temporarily with their grandma Bartlow and dad where they could continue attending school would be the best choice... I left with a decision to save my life, and then to come back and get my children.

I thank God for Ms. Bartlow. She never let me down and always had my back. So there I was living at my sister's house so shamefaced and depressed, still trying to find my way. I wasn't using drugs but I was still in pain. She never made me feel bad or unwanted there. It was the guilt of having been on drugs. Being the eldest of all seven of us, and now I was sleeping on my baby sister's couch, added another layer of humiliation.

I remember when we first got to Sacramento. She did my hair, bought me clothes, and took care of me. One(no comma here) thing for sure, I didn't lose was my desire to dress and keep myself up no matter what, and my sister knew I liked this. She's a wonderful sister who cared for me and helped me feel better about myself.e There was a day I was on the phone with my kids' kids father. He told me I couldn't get my children. I was livid. I mean we never kept the kids from each other., I didn't know at the time, but he had connected with the girl he cheated on me with. He had gotten clean just before me, ran into Meshawn, and they got together while I was finding me. She was so evil. I found out things she did while she was in my children's company.

Long story short, I remember going to her job one day in Emeryville before we started using drugs. My babies were so little, like three and four I made her get in my van and I took her to cash her check. I took her money, drove to 96th B St., Twhere BD was, put her out of the car, and left her ass there! I couldn't believe the rumors were true. I was being told that my baby's daddy was cheating on me with a girl that looked just like me. They said she was a cute girl with beautiful brown skin, a cute hairstyle, a small waist, and shorts like me. But guess what? I felt I had it going on with two babies back to back; I still looked snatched! So, one day I was riding with my cousin Tanesha.

As we were coming up 98th we found out the rumors everyone was talking about were true! They were sitting outside the wash house talking. I drove up behind his car. They jumped in his ride, and pulled off fast!!! I couldn't wait to see his ass. I couldn't believe I had two young babies by this nigga and he was cheating on me!! I had to be like 23 or 24. He was all I had besides my children. He was the only person I had ever trusted and he had betrayed me? This shit hit my soul deeply. I lost it. He told me he wouldn't do it again. And this is the same woman that conveniently ran into him, the kid's father when I left with my sister.

They were dating and playing house with my babies! I felt betrayed again. I had it in my head that when I went to Sacramento that I would get it together. I would be back, and get my family back also.

Well, years later my sister told me that BD had called and told her he was about to go to Reno and was going to marry Meshawn!!! Sister never told me when he actually called to announce it. She thought she was protecting me from him. I never found out until years later what happened. Not being aware of my destiny hurt to the core. I'm not sure if my sister truly understood how much I loved her for loving me that much to protect me from the news that would break my heart at that crucial point in my life.

After they got married, shit just went downhill. I kind of thought this woman was the devil. Did she poison my BD? He had never been so evil to me until he got with her. We never had custody issues. We shared OUR babies. Now he was telling me when and how I could see the children I bore!! No one told me I had to get full or joint custody. What was I supposed to do? I had worked hard to regain myself so I could raise my kids in a loving, healthy drug-free environment and now this?

The man I just knew was my angel sent from my grandma Lois was now ripping my soul into pieces. He allowed this woman to raise my children as if they were hers and just made me exempt to appease her? I was lost. Then at the perfect time, my sister said fuck this! And helped me find out how to get the kids back! I walked into that courtroom and this woman had the courts thinking so badly of me. BD and I were both recovered addicts. Why were they making me look so bad? They even made me visit my children in front of this white woman. She was a court-appointed mediator!

I couldn't believe after leaving to get myself together for my children that I deserved this. After a few of those supervised meetings, I went to visit my children at a different location in Hayward... This time I had a Mexican woman as our mediator. **She** saw how my children and I were chilling. She saw we didn't belong there. She let us leave. Lo and behold this was my escape. Again, neither one of us had full custody! So I hit 580 to the 80 East and drove my children back to Sacramento, enrolled them in school, and kept it pushing.

We were staying in my sister's house until my move-in date came through. It had been six months since we were in our new home when I figured I could tell BD where we were, so he could come to see his babies. I had purchased everything brand new. They had custom bunk beds because it was a cute two-bedroom place just for us. I decorated it as if it was the big home I'd dreamed of. I told him where we were. His brother Johnathan and his father Paul (rest in paradise to both of the; I loved those two.) came with him...

It was lil' Jay's birthday party. They ate, fellowshipped, and without my knowledge, they plotted to steal my kids back. When I called my sister I was In complete despair! tears flowing down my face I could barely speak. My sister, Q started yelling, "Why the fuck did you tell him where you live"?

She was pissed, she had told me not to trust BD. She was seeing clearly while I was truly wanting my children to see their daddy. I remember how they snatched my kids, as my daughter was in the backseat yelling towards the back windshield banging on that window, and screaming for me. It hurts to even remember or hear that scream. It ripped me right back into pieces that night. I couldn't sleep. I looked at my sister and she said, "Let's go get my kids"!

We drove down 580 to Oakland, pulled up, and watched the house. Then I decided to call the police. When the police arrived they went into the house and came out. They told me, "Ma'am, your kids are not in danger. Plus they're with their dad. There's absolutely nothing we can do"!!

I was furious with myself, because I was betrayed by the police at age seven-now they were doing it again. When they left, my sister and I created a plan deciding we were not leaving without them.! We slept in the car until daylight. Instead of me running in to get my babies, my sister said she would go in after BD dropped them off at school. As soon as we saw him walking back home my sister ran in and it seemed like within seconds she came running out with my babies!!!

I remember smiling so hard. I was so happy to have gotten them back. I couldn't rest until they were with me. I dreamed of raising my children and being married to one man. This was very important to me due to what I saw Momma go through over the years. I just wanted that white picket fence. At seven years, old momma had six baby daddies and seven children. I kept telling myself not me. I feel like it's why I stayed in fucked up relationships. Momma on the other hand said fuck them niggas.

18

It didn't happen the way I dreamed. It happened exactly how the universe needed it to be. I have not one regret. The worst thing you could do is try to do things for others.

The whole time I was trying to live a life satisfying others. So guess what? I relapsed. When I decided to stand up for myself, I never turned back.

That was the day I fell in love with myself. That day I walked into my sister Qu's house and started screaming thank you, Jesus!!!! I was so determined to get off the drugs, to start living, not just exist. Since then I've had some adversities, trials, and tribulations.

I chose to share my story in hopes of someone else being uplifted and encouraged that they're not alone. I had swept all the hurt and pain from my childhood under the rug, and that itself wasn't healthy. I've found myself continuing that path, and now I realize it's a very unhealthy pattern that needs to be broken. I have decided to wake up and finish this journey of healing.

No one is obligated to heal you but you. Even though I've been delivered from drugs, I found myself drinking way too much, in denial until I met King in October of 2020.

This man has changed my life! Up until November 29th, 2021, I didn't know how much of an indulging problem I had. It was a late birthday celebration which was 11/22, and King and I were out of the country. When we returned, my sister had gathered up the ladies to celebrate with me. I was at King's house and had to drive down from Richmond to Sacramento. We went and got a yoni cleansing, then had an early dinner. King drove down for dinner. I had been having a great time with the ladies, not realizing I had drunk way too much!

As we wrapped up dinner we then headed to play pool. I was tipsy as hell, unaware of what was happening. When I woke up the next day King wasn't home with me. I was devastated! Also, I was still in denial thinking why is it that every time I drink around him it's a problem? But if he had come I would've had a great time and would probably still be in denial to this day. But baby…King doesn't play! He told me he left that night because I was so disrespectful. I had called him everything under the sun. I was ashamed of my behavior. I loved, adored, and respected him. How could I treat him in that manner? On the 30th I looked myself in the mirror and said, ``No more Lois''!!!

Since 1/13/22, I haven't had not one cocktail, besides a little glass of wine. I was finding myself drinking fifths with people and not knowing how to drink socially. It was disgusting! How could I lose myself and the man I prayed for?

Something had to give, so on that day, I knew if I did the work on myself the universe would send the King back to me. King came back! Since meeting King I have traveled more than I ever have in the entire 47 years of my life. I've been the happiest I've ever been. He walked into my life during a period when he said after his wife, he'd never fall in love again. Meeting him was truly a blessing. The way he looks at me and the way he treats me is everything.

Since that day he came to my home and got out of the car with those beautiful smelling flowers for his goddess, me, it's been heaven. As he approached me, it was this feeling that I still can't manage to explain. It's a feeling that I had prayed for on that winter day. I prayed it would never go away. We're on our 14th month together, and when I tell you that feeling is still there, I kid you not. He can look at me, and I feel it. He can just be walking toward me, and I feel it. When he touches my hand the feeling is still there.

I'm still crazy in love with this man, and I look forward to the day I walk down that aisle and marry him. You see when you get out of your own way and allow the universe to bless your love life and life period as you love yourself, everything will fall into place.

Thank you universe.

ABOUT THE AUTHOR:

Lois Milikini is a remarkable woman who has overcome numerous obstacles to become the successful person she is today. Born in Pomona, California, she was raised in Oakland as the oldest of seven siblings. From a young age, Lois faced many challenges, including abuse both as a child and later as an adult. She struggled with drug addiction for many years, but after 21 years of being clean, she has turned her life around.

Lois began her career as a hairstylist and eventually became a highly respected personal stylist, helping people feel confident and beautiful in their own skin. She also offers body contouring services to help people feel comfortable and proud of their bodies. Her passion for helping people extends beyond just their physical appearance; she is also an advocate for mental health and wellness.

In addition to her successful career, Lois is a proud mother of two adult children. She has written a book called "Mask Off," in which she shares her personal story of overcoming abuse and addiction. The book is intended to inspire and encourage women who are going through similar struggles, reminding them that they too can find freedom and healing.

Lois Milikini is an inspiration to many, proving that no matter what challenges life may throw your way, it is possible to overcome them and find happiness and success.

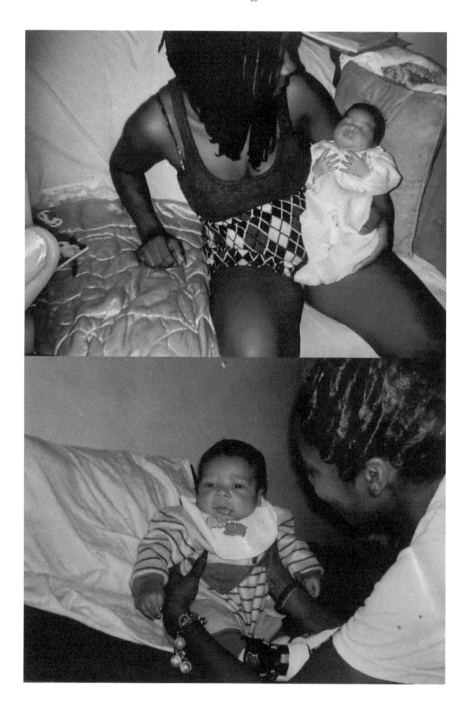

CPSIA information can be obtained
at www.ICGtesting.com
Printed in the USA
LVHW080915270523
748234LV00008B/50